Linda H

Linda H

Marmaduke's Maths

Shape

Karen Bryant-Mole

Evans

Marmaduke's Maths

Counting • Pattern • Shape • Size
Sorting • Where is Marmaduke?

Published by Evans Brothers Limited
2A Portman Mansions
Chiltern Street
London W1M 1LE

© BryantMole Books 1999

First published in 1999

Printed in Hong Kong by Wing King Tong Co Ltd

British Library Cataloguing in Publication Data

Bryant-Mole, Karen
  Shape. - (Marmaduke's Maths)
  1.Marmaduke (Fictitious character) - Juvenile literature
  2.Geometrical constructions - Juvenile literature
  3.Form perception - Juvenile literature
  I.Title
  516.1'5

  ISBN 0237519046

Created by Karen Bryant-Mole
Photographed by Zul Mukhida
Designed by Jean Wheeler
Teddy bear by Merrythought Ltd

About this book

Marmaduke the teddy helps children to understand mathematical concepts by guiding them through the learning process in a fun, friendly way.

This book introduces children to the concept of shape. Children are introduced to the idea that there are two different types of shape, 2D and 3D, and are taught how individual shapes can be defined. Everyday examples help children to recognise these shapes.

You can use this book as a starting point for further work on shape. It is very important that shape words are used correctly. Objects that are described in 2D terms must be flat. Balls are not circles, they are spheres. Look out for shapes all around you. Kitchen cupboards are good places to find cubes, cuboids and cylinders. Watch out for road signs in the shape of circles, rectangles and triangles.

contents

shapes

Marmaduke is cutting out some shapes from coloured paper.

Paper is very thin.
All the shapes are flat.

Flat shapes are sometimes called 2D shapes.

Marmaduke's bricks are not flat.
Shapes that are not flat are called solid shapes.

Solid shapes can also be called 3D shapes.

circle

Marmaduke is
wearing a big badge.

The shape of
my badge is called
a circle.

Circles are flat shapes.
They have no corners.
They have one curved side that
goes all the way round.

All of these things are circles.

some buttons

a biscuit

some coins

rectangle

Marmaduke has been sent a postcard.

The shape of this postcard is a rectangle.

Rectangles are flat shapes.
They have four corners and four straight sides.

Here are some more rectangles.

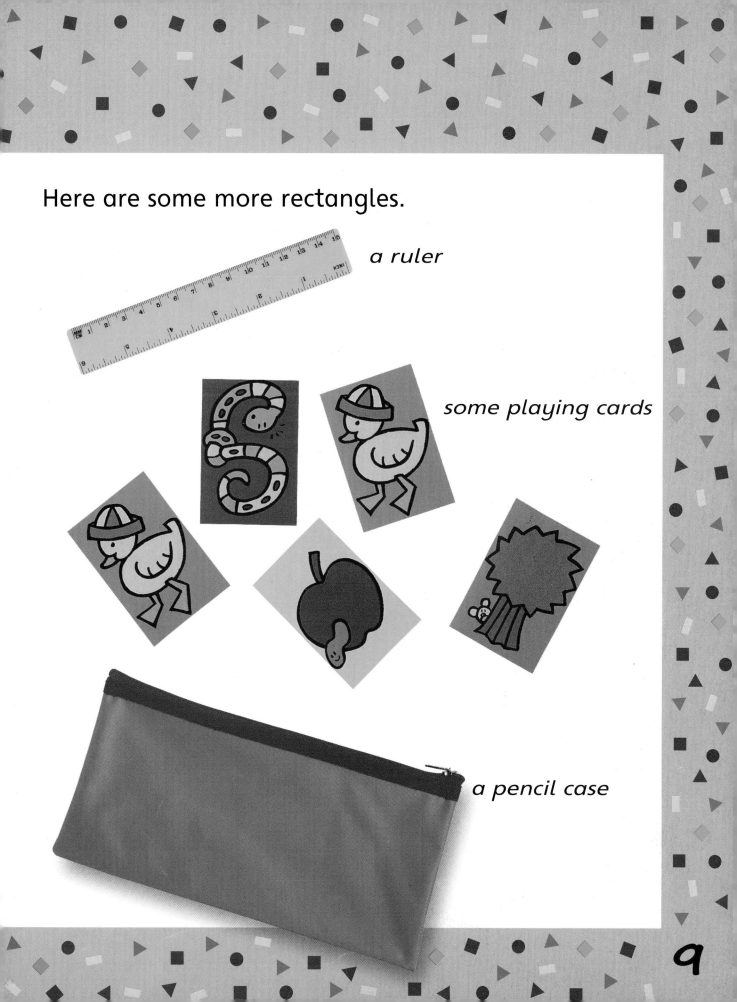

a ruler

some playing cards

a pencil case

square

Marmaduke is going to wash some dishes.
He is holding a dishcloth.

The shape of my dishcloth is a square.

Squares are special rectangles.
All the sides are the same length.

Here are some more squares
that Marmaduke found
around his home.

a flannel

a duster

a paper serviette

triangle

Marmaduke is waving a flag.

The shape of this flag is a triangle.

Triangles are flat shapes. They have three straight sides and three corners.

These shapes are all triangles but
they all look very different.
Count the sides and the corners.

sphere

Marmaduke is holding a blue ball.

The shape of this ball is a sphere.

Spheres are solid shapes.
They are perfectly round.
Spheres roll very easily.

Here are some more balls.
They are all spheres but
they are different sizes.

cylinder

Marmaduke has been shopping.
He bought a tin of fruit.

The shape of this tin is called a cylinder.

Cylinders are solid shapes.
They are like tubes with closed ends.

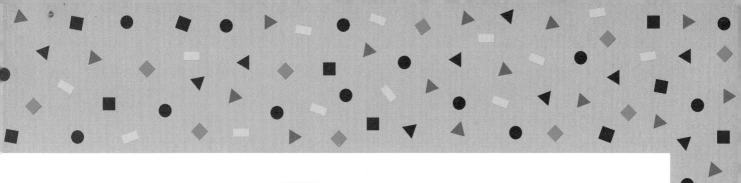

Here are some more cylinders that Marmaduke bought at the shops.

cuboid

It is Marmaduke's birthday.
He has been given
a present.

The shape of
this present is called
a cuboid.

Cuboids are solid shapes.
Some sides of a cuboid are longer than others.

Here are some
more presents.
They are
all cuboids.

cube

Poor Marmaduke has a cold.
He has a box of tissues.

The shape of the box is a cube.

Cubes are solid shapes.
All their sides are the same length.

Here are some more cubes.

*some
wooden bricks*

some sweets

two dice

Which is which?

Marmaduke is trying to remember the names of all the shapes.

Can you help me?

If you cannot remember, look back through the book.
Marmaduke has already shown you each of these objects.

glossary

dice cubes with different numbers of dots on their sides, thrown in board games

flannel sometimes called a face cloth

playing cards cards used to play card games, such as Snap and Pairs

ruler an object used to measure how long things are

serviette an object used to wipe your mouth or fingers when you are eating a meal

tissues paper handkerchiefs that are thrown away after they have been used

index